With love to Lesley xmas '82.

From, Uncle Lewis Auntie Greta.

The Christmas Book

Macdonald Educational

Written and planned by
Susan Baker

Managing Editor
Mary Tapissier

Cover illustration
Peter Dennis

Illustrators
Frank Baber
pages 4-5, 8-9, 12-13, 16-17,
24-25, 36-37, 44-45
Kim Blundell
pages 20-21, 30-31, 34-35,
38, 40-41
Sara Cole
pages 6-7, 10-11, 18
22-23, 28-29, 32-33, 42-43
Peter Dennis
pages 14-15, 39, 46-47

Fiction
page 16, The First Christmas
©Richard Blythe 1978
page 39, A Christmas King in a
Paper Crown© Richard Blythe 1978

Advisory Panel
Margot Lindsay, librarian
Margaret Payne, teacher

First published 1978
Second impression 1979
Third impression 1980
Revised edition 1981
Macdonald & Co. (Publishers) Ltd.
Holywell House
Worship St
London EC2

Printed and bound by
New Interlitho, Milan, Italy

Contents

The First Santa Claus

Christmas is the time of year when we celebrate the birth day of Christ. The church is lit with candles for the Christmas service—the Christ Mass. Carol singers go from house to house. People kiss under the mistletoe and shake hands as a sign of friendship. We hang up evergreens in our houses and decorate trees with glittering ornaments and lights. We have a special Christmas dinner and then pull crackers, dress up in paper hats and play games. And most exciting of all, we give presents, just as the shepherds and kings gave presents to the new-born child in Bethlehem, nearly two thousand years ago.

Dutch children do not have to wait until Christmas Day for all their presents. On December 6, which is St Nicholas' Day, they are visited by a kind old gentleman with a long white beard. He is dressed like a bishop in a long red cape with a mitre on his head and a crook in his hand. He comes from Spain in a sailing ship. Crowds of children dress up in their national costumes and greet him in Amsterdam.

St Nicholas rides on a white horse to visit each house where he asks the parents if their children have been good. One of his attendants writes down the answer in a book. That night, the children fill their wooden clogs or shoes with carrots for his horse. They put them beside the big kitchen stove, or on the window sill. Next morning, good children find the carrots gone and their shoes filled with sweets and little presents. Very naughty children find only a bunch of sticks for beating them with!

The first St Nicholas was a bishop over a thousand years ago. He once saved the lives of some children, and he was a very good man, so he became the patron saint of all children.

St Nicholas visits children in other countries too. When the Dutch settlers went to America three hundred years ago they spread the tradition of their St Nicholas, or Santa Klaus as they called him. That is how we get the name Santa Claus. In America, his white horse disappeared and he now rides in a sleigh pulled by reindeer.

Advent Calendar

During the month before Christmas everyone is busy getting everything ready. The traditional time for making cakes and puddings was Stir-Up Sunday at the end of November. Next comes Advent Sunday. In Germany they hang up Advent wreaths of holly with four red candles in the centre. They light one candle each Sunday and the last on Christmas Eve. Children count the days until Christmas using an Advent calendar. They open one window each day and find a Christmas picture inside. Why not make one of your own!

You will need

brush
paints
scissors
paper
card
crayons
pencil
glue
old cards, scraps, stamps or seals

1. Draw a picture on card with 23 little windows and one big one.

2. Paint the picture. Number each window. Let the paint dry.

3. Collect little pictures to fit inside each window. Use scraps cut from old cards, stamps, seals—or draw your own pictures.

4. Paste the pictures inside the windows. The last big window is usually a nativity scene.

5. Cut some small squares of paper to fit over the windows like shutters. Glue them on at one side.

6. Use crayons to colour in the window covers when the glue is dry.

Start using your calendar on December 1st. Open one window each day.

Our calendar shows the children in this house getting ready for Christmas. They are keeping Christmas traditions from many countries, so they have something different to do every day.

Here are some other suggestions for calendar pictures – a village, a ship, a block of flats, a Christmas tree.

Evergreens

Many of our Christmas customs began thousands of years before Christ was born, when people worshipped the Sun. The Sun gave them heat and light which they needed to stay alive. Every winter the days get shorter until mid December, when they begin to lengthen again. This was the time for a celebration when the people could look forward to the end of winter and the coming of spring. In northern countries the festival was called Yule. It was a time for feasting, singing, dancing and other noisy entertainments.

Evergreens, which are plants that keep their leaves and even produce flowers and fruit, throughout the winter, seemed magical to these people. In northern countries, when they cleaned their houses for the winter festival, they took sweet-smelling pine branches, rosemary and other evergreens into the houses to lay on the damp floors and decorate the walls.

Most important of all was the yule log, the biggest log that could be found, perhaps a whole tree root. This was dragged home in a procession and laid in the huge open fireplace to give heat and light during the festival. It would be lit on Christmas Eve and kept burning for days. Some people kept a piece of each year's log and put it on the fire the following year.

Nowadays, the most important decoration is the Christmas tree. Queen Victoria's husband Prince Albert brought the first Christmas tree to Windsor Castle in 1834 for the royal family. Many other families in England soon copied this German tradition.

All these plants are traditional evergreens, except Poinsettia which is now a popular indoor plant at Christmas.

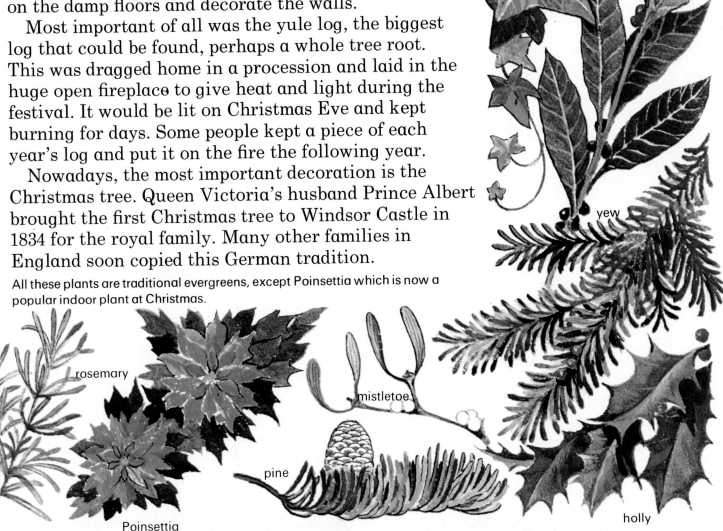

Christmas rose

bay laurel

ivy

yew

rosemary

mistletoe

pine

Poinsettia

holly

Christmas Cards

Christmas cards became popular just over a hundred years ago. The first ones were decorated with flowers and looked rather like birthday cards. Christmas scenes with robins, holly, snow scenes and people dressed in their best winter clothes came later. Nativity scenes, angels and other religious pictures also became popular. We still send cards like these as well as modern designs.

Some cards were very elaborate, with pop-up pictures and moving parts. Here are two ways of making some extra special Christmas cards.

A Christmas Piece.
Children copied out prayers or wrote Christmas greetings to their parents on pieces of decorated card.

Pop-up card. You will need

ruler
crayons
glue
scissors
stiff paper

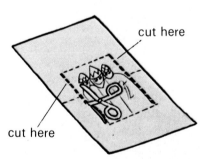

1. Cut two pieces of paper about 20cm by 30cm. Fold them in half then open them out flat.

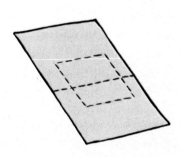

2. Inside one piece, draw a square in the middle about 10cm by 10cm.

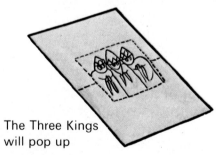

The Three Kings will pop up

3. Draw a picture on it with the part you want to pop up inside the square.

cut here
cut here

4. Cut along the two sides of the square (along the red dotted lines).

cut here
do not cut here

5. Cut round the top of your pop-up but do not cut the 'shoulders' at the sides.

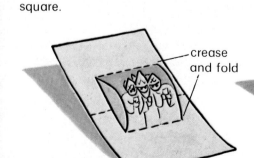

crease and fold

6. Crease and fold forwards along the top and bottom of the square (along the blue dotted lines).

crease and fold

7. Crease the shoulders (blue dotted lines) and fold them backwards.

glue at edge only

8. Use glue at the edges to stick the pop-up inside the second piece of folded paper.

10

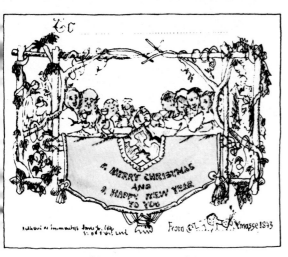

Victorian Christmas cards

This was one of the very first Christmas cards, designed in 1843

Pictures of the Christmas mail coach are still popular

The Victorians were fond of sad pictures of robins which reminded them of the cold and hungry.

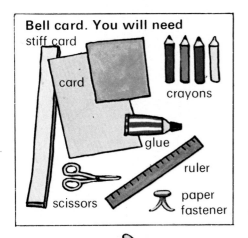

Bell card. You will need

stiff card

card

crayons

glue

ruler

scissors

paper fastener

1. Draw a bell 5cm high on card. Colour it and cut it out.

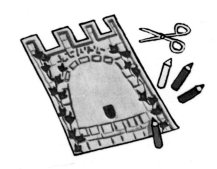

2. Draw a background for the bell on piece of card 10cm by 10cm. Colour it. Write a Christmas message.

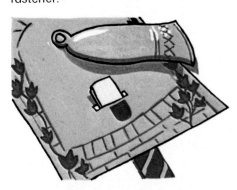

3. Fix the top of the bell to the background card with a paper fastener.

lever

4. Cut a narrow strip of stiff card 10cm long to make a lever. Colour one end to look like a bell rope.

slit

5. Make a slit across the background card behind the bell.

6. Push the plain end of the lever through the slit from behind the card.

7. Hold lever and bell straight. Lift the bell and glue tip of lever to back of bell.

8. When glue is dry, move 'rope' lever gently from side to side to make bell swing.

Carol Singers

Christmas is a time for visiting friends and relations, settling quarrels and giving presents.

In many countries children walk from house to house singing carols and wishing everybody a happy Christmas. Curtains are not drawn so that the light from the windows is a welcoming sign to travellers and visitors.

In Mexico people dress up and go in procession to visit each house in memory of Mary and Joseph's search for a place to stay in Bethlehem.

In Germany and Austria the children go around on the Thursday before Christmas making a lot of noise with bells, whistles and drums. Some of them dress up in ugly masks and chase people. This is because of the old superstition that the dark winter nights are haunted by evil goblins, ghosts and trolls. The noise and the masks are supposed to frighten evil spirits away.

On Christmas Eve the church bells ring for the midnight service. In the snowy mountain villages there are beautiful strings of flickering lights all over the mountainsides as people make their way to church by torchlight.

On the eve of January 6 children dress up as the Three Kings and carry a star round the houses, singing carols. There are Star Singers in many European countries.

In England, the carol singers used to be called wassail singers because their cry of greeting was 'wassail' meaning 'be whole' or 'good health'. They would be invited into each house and given cakes or mince pies and a warm drink from the wassail bowl. One type of drink was called lambswool. It was made from spiced ale with roasted apples.

Carol singers nowadays usually collect money to give away to a charity. But in the days when many people worked on farms, there was no work in the middle of winter and their families were often cold and hungry. Wassailing rich people was a way of getting some warm food and drink and wishing their masters good health at the same time. In one part of Germany the singers pushed a pitchfork through the doorway, expecting food to be stuck on the prongs for them to take away.

12

The Fir Tree

In a sunny forest clearing stood a pretty little Fir Tree. It was a beautiful part of the forest but the Tree often wished it could go away somewhere else.

'Hush,' whispered the breeze, 'You should be happy living in such a lovely place.'

In summer, children came gathering strawberries. 'What a pretty little tree!' they cried. But the Tree just wished that it could grow bigger and see the world across the tree tops.

In winter, when the snow lay all around, a friendly hare jumped right over the little Tree. The Tree was very indignant and was pleased when, after a few seasons, it grew taller so that the hare had to run around it.

In the autumn, woodcutters came and felled the tallest trees, cutting off all the branches and carting the long trunks away on waggons.

'I wonder where they are going?' thought the little Tree.

In the spring, it asked the swallows and the stork if they knew where the tall trees had gone.

'I think they were made into the masts for ships that sail across the sea,' said the stork.

'I wish I could go across the sea. Do tell me about it,' begged the Tree. But the stork had no time to explain, and it flew away.

At Christmas time, more woodcutters came and took away whole young trees on their carts.

'I wish I could ride on a cart,' grumbled the Tree. 'Look at that one! It is smaller than I am. Why have they been chosen?'

'We know where they go. We know!' twittered the sparrows. 'We've been to town and looked through the windows of the big houses. Each tree stands in the best room with glittering decorations hung all over it.'

'I wish that could happen to me,' sighed the Tree — and the very next Christmas it did!

At first the Tree was sorry to leave its forest friends behind. But when it arrived at a huge house and was set up in the best room, it was very proud. Beautiful decorations hung all over it. There were little bags of fruit and nuts painted silver and gold, sweets and biscuits, pretty dolls and little toys. Red, white and blue candles were fastened to its branches and a glittering star was fixed at the very top.

'I wonder if the sparrows will see me and tell my friends how fine I look?' thought the conceited Tree.

In the evening the candles were lit. The Tree trembled so much with excitement that one of its toys caught fire. Someone quickly put out the flames and the frightened Tree kept quite still after that.

Everyone in the house stood and admired the tree. At first the little children were speechless, but then they rushed up to it, shrieking with delight, and took down all the gifts and decorations from the branches.

The Tree was quite alarmed and nearly toppled over as the children pulled it about.

When all the presents had been shared out, the children came and sat beneath the tree to listen to an old man who told them a story. It was the tale of Humpty Dumpty and the Tree listened, spellbound, for it had never heard a storyteller before.

Eventually the party finished and the candles were safely put out. The room was quiet at last and the Tree wondered what would happen next.

'I expect they will dress me up all over again, tomorrow,' it thought. But instead, the servants came and took the Tree down. They pushed it into a dark, dusty corner up in the attic. All that was left of the decorations was the star. The Tree felt lonely and

forgotten and it began to remember its forest home with the birds, the crisp white snow and the playful hare.

One day, some nosey mice crept out and scampered in the Tree's branches.

'Where do you come from, old tree?' they asked, cheekily.

'I'm not all that old,' the Tree protested. 'Only last year I was growing in a beautiful forest.'

'Oh do tell us,' begged the mice. So the Tree told them about the happy days it had spent growing up among the flowers and the birds with the other trees.

The mice listened, fascinated. 'How happy you must have been,' they said.

'Oh! I was happiest when I came here,' the Tree told them. And it described the splendid party and the Christmas candles on its branches.

'Candles! We love eating those,' squeaked the mice. 'Tell us more!'

'I could tell you a story,' the Tree suggested.

'Yes, do tell us a story,' the mice begged.

So the Tree repeated the story of Humpty Dumpty that it had heard that Christmas Day.

The next night, the mice brought more friends with them to listen to the Tree. But when the Tree began telling the story of Humpty Dumpty all over again, some of the mice were bored to hear it a second time.

'Don't you know any storeroom stories — about candles and things to eat?' the mice asked.

The Tree confessed that it did not know any other stories at all. The mice lost interest and scampered away to play somewhere else.

After a very long time, people came to tidy up the attic. Someone dragged the Tree out and took it downstairs. A few of its branches were broken because they had grown so dry and brittle, but the Tree was pleased to be taken out again.

'Now I shall be decorated and put in the big room again,' the Tree thought.

But the servants just threw it out into the garden, and the children clambered over it, breaking more of the branches.

'Look what's stuck on the ugly old tree!' shouted a little boy, grabbing the star off the top.

'Am I really old and ugly?' wondered

the Tree, only just realising how brown and withered its branches were.

A gardener chopped the tree up and put it on a bonfire. The children watched the needles crackle and splutter in the heat. The little boy wore the star whilst the Tree sighed sadly. It remembered that Christmas Day and all the other happy days in the forest with the birds and even the cold attic nights with the mice.

But all those days were gone and now the Tree's life had come to an end and this story must end too.

The First Christmas

Once upon a time, nearly two thousand years ago, a carpenter named Joseph made a difficult journey. The ruler of Rome said that all the people of his empire must be taxed, so Joseph and his wife went to a town where the tax-gatherers could write down their names.

It was the coldest time of winter. Joseph walked all the way, and his wife, who was called Mary, rode on their donkey. Mary was going to have a baby, so Joseph had to take great care of her.

When they arrived at the town, which was called Bethlehem, Mary and Joseph found that every inn was already full. Mary knew her baby was to be born very soon, but there was nowhere for them to go. The only place where they might shelter was a stable.

That same night, on a hill near Bethlehem, some shepherds were keeping guard over their sheep when a strange and wonderful thing happened. It seemed as if all the cold hillside suddenly blazed with light. The Shepherds did not know it, but at that moment, in Bethlehem, Mary's baby was born.

The shepherds were frightened. The light around them grew brighter. Their ears were filled with sound, as if the stars themselves were singing. Each fell to his knees, certain that all that blaze and brilliance must come from God. They seemed to hear voices in the light, telling them to go to Bethlehem to find a new-born king.

In the icy darkness, they stumbled down the hill, dazed and scarcely knowing where they went. They reached Bethlehem just before dawn. All was cold and silent, but they saw a light, a lantern, shining in a stable. They went, and looked inside.

Joseph and Mary were kneeling there, beside a cattle-manger where a baby lay, warmly wrapped.

Joseph beckoned. 'This is the Prince of Heaven,' he said, 'sent to us to comfort men and guide them to God.'

Mary's eyes glistened with tears. She stroked the cheek of the sleeping child, saying,

'This is my dear son. His name is Jesus.'

All the stable seemed to glow with light, and on that first Christmas morning the shepherds, too, knelt before Mary's son and bowed down in wonder.

16   **by Richard Blythe**

Christmas Crib

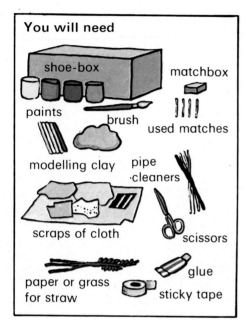

shoe-box | matchbox
paints | used matches
brush
modelling clay | pipe cleaners
scraps of cloth | scissors
paper or grass for straw | glue | sticky tape

1. Paint a shoe box to look like the stable.

2. Make people from pipe cleaners or modelling clay. Dress them in cloth scraps.

3. Make animals from pipe cleaners or clay.

4. Make manger from matchbox. Cut it in half to make a trough. Stick on match legs.

In Spanish and Italian homes the crib is the most important part of the Christmas decorations.

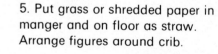

5. Put grass or shredded paper in manger and on floor as straw. Arrange figures around crib.

Christmas Decorations

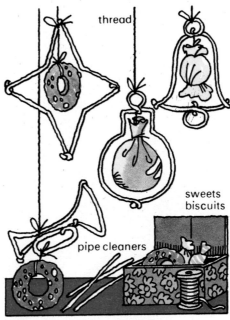

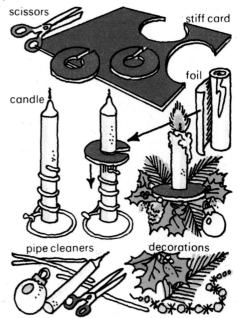

Parrot Mobile

Trace parrot onto card. Colour it and cut it out. (Make sure the slot is slightly smaller than the matches.) Make perches from **used matches**. Make perch holders from pipe cleaners. Make a few more. Tie one completed parrot perch at each end of a straight pipe cleaner. Tie them all together with more thread and hang up your mobile.

Christmas Tree Gifts

Bend the pipe cleaners into pretty shapes. Hang sweets or biscuits by thread inside the shapes. You can use anything that is small for a tree gift like this. Use your imagination for other shapes.

Christmas Candle Holders

Use small candles. Twist a pipe cleaner round a candle, make sure it is firm. Cut some card rings out and cover them with foil. Fit them on the candles to catch the molten wax. **Get an adult to light the candles.**

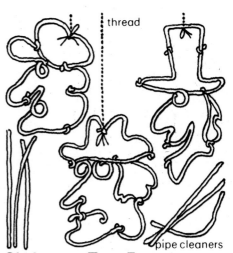

Catch Father Christmas!

Make some Father Christmases out of stiff card and colour them. Glue stands onto them. Make some rings out of pipe cleaners and start throwing!

Christmas Tree Faces

You can make all sorts of strange and funny faces from pipe cleaners. Hang them on your Christmas tree with pretty thread.

Christmas Presents

Father Christmas

La Befana

Christkindl

Giving presents is a way of showing people that you like them. Long ago people used to give each other presents of candles and dolls during the winter festival. Now we give presents as a reminder of the Christmas message. 'Peace on earth and good will to all men'.

The most exciting presents are the children's toys.

In England, Father Christmas delivers them during the night before Christmas. The children leave an empty stocking or pillowcase hanging at the end of the bed. In the morning they hope it will be full of presents.

In Germany the traditional visitor is the Christkindl who is the Christ Child's messenger. She is a beautiful fair-haired girl with a shining crown of candles who visits each house with a basket of presents. In some German homes a room is locked up before Christmas. On Christmas Eve the children go to bed but are woken up at midnight by their parents and taken down to the locked room. The door is opened and they see the tree all lit up, with piles of parcels on little tables.

In Scandinavia a little gnome called Julenisse puts the presents under the Christmas tree in the night. The children leave a bowl of porridge out for him. In Russia someone called Grandfather Frost brings children presents in December.

In Spain and Italy the children wait until Epiphany, January 6, for their presents. In Spain they are brought by the Three Kings on their camels. The children go out in the evening to look for them but no one has ever managed to catch sight of them. So they put their shoes on the window sill or balcony, with some straw for the camels, before they go to bed. Next morning they find presents there, just like the Dutch children do after a visit from St Nicholas.

La Befana, the kind witch, brings the presents to Italian children on January 6. She was a woman who followed the wise men but got lost. She has been wandering Italy ever since, giving presents to children at Christmas.

On the day after Christmas people give tradesmen money. In England this is called Boxing Day because boys used to go round collecting money in clay boxes. When the boxes were full, they broke them open.

Julenisse

Grandfather Frost

The Three Kings

St Nicholas

Tree Decorations

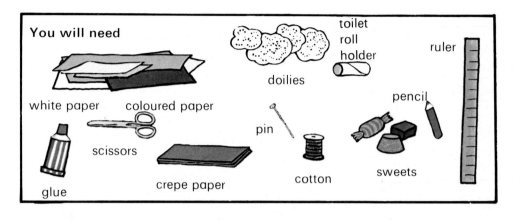

white paper · coloured paper · doilies · toilet roll holder · ruler · pencil · pin · cotton · sweets · glue · scissors · crepe paper

Twisted Chains

1. Cut a long paper strip 5cm wide from a roll of crepe paper.

2. Fold strip up like a concertina. Cut pattern round edge.

3. Unfold it. Twist it round and round. Fasten it up at the ends.

Ring Chains

1. Cut 20 strips of coloured paper 3cm wide and 15cm long.

2. Make one ring. Glue ends.

3. Slip next strip through. Make ring. Glue ends. Use up all the strips like this.

Folded Chains

1. Cut two long narrow strips of paper 2cm wide.

2. Lay ends together. Fold strips over each other in turn as in A, B, C and D.

3. Glue on more strips to make chain longer. Glue down last end.

Crackers

 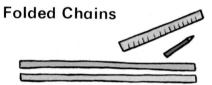 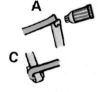 

1. Fill toilet roll holder with sweets. Roll up in paper.

2. Glue edge and tie ends with cotton.

3. Trim ends and fan out.

Heart Baskets

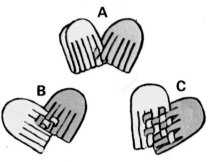
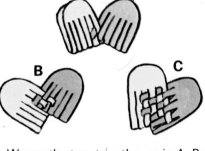

1. Cut these shapes out of two folded bits of paper. Cuts slits across the folds. Make the slits slightly longer than the width of the paper.

2. Weave the two together as in A, B and C. Each strip goes inside and then outside the different coloured strips. Carry on until all the strips are woven together.

3. Open heart-shaped basket. Glue on handle. Hang up.

Snowflakes

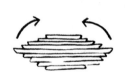

1. Cut circle of white paper. Trim round edge.

2. Fold up like a concertina.

3. Pull two ends round and glue.

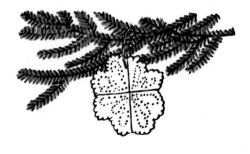

4. Make another the same. Glue sides together. Hang up with thread.

5. Glue 3 together to make 6-pointed star.

6. Use doilies to make them too.

Fasting and Feasting

Roast turkey, plum pudding, mince pies and Christmas cake make an enormous meal. Not so very long ago, many people did not get enough to eat during most of the winter. By December, most of the store of hay and corn would be used up and the animals which had lived on it had to be slaughtered. Then people could look forward to a feast at Christmas.

In many countries people kept pigs which were fattened up for Christmas. The boar's head was served with an apple in its mouth and a garland of rosemary. Some people roasted a whole pig on a spit. Others had just a joint of pork or a cured ham. In Austria pork was made into special sausages.

Everywhere, people tried to give themselves a treat and have something special to eat. Roast goose was popular in England but now most people have roast turkey. Peacock used to be served, with all its feathers put back over it after it was cooked. In Scandinavia they eat roasted pork ribs, salted cod and a special rice

pudding. In countries a long way from the sea, fish is a special treat and is the main dish at Christmas.

In England, Christmas dinner was usually eaten at midday on December 25, during daylight. In Spain, families had their meal immediately after Midnight Mass on Christmas Eve. In Finland the meal was begun as soon as the first star appeared in the sky.

In every country it was usual to fast, or starve, before the feast. In England, the only thing that people ate on the day before the feast was frumenty. This was a kind of porridge made from corn. Over the years the recipe changed. Eggs, fruit, spices, lumps of meat and dried plums were added. The whole mixture was wrapped in a cloth and boiled. This is how plum pudding began. Nowadays we put in more fruit instead of meat. Mince pies also used to contain meat.

Christmas feasts have always included nuts, fruit, sweets, cakes and biscuits. Gingerbread men and animals are popular gifts in many countries.

Table Decorations

You will need

paints
coloured paper
stiff card
glue
brush
pencil
scissors
decorations

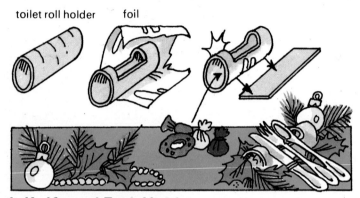

toilet roll holder   foil

1. Knife and Fork Holder

Cut a hole in toilet roll holder so a knife, fork and spoon can rest on it. Wrap foil round it. Cut piece of card the length and width of roll. Glue it to roll. Fill roll with nuts or sweets. Decorate with holly and fir and your holder is ready.

2. Table Mats

Fold coloured paper in half and in half again. Cut edge with pretty pattern. Unfold it. Cut out pictures from magazines and stick them on. You could also draw your own pictures.

3. Bowl Decorations

You can decorate bowls by cutting strips of coloured paper in pretty patterns.

4. Christmas Nut Bowl

Cut stiff card circle about 20cm across. Cover with foil. Cut out foil circles about 5 times the candle thickness. Wrap foil round candle bottom. Pull top of foil down to finish candle holder. Stick holders **firmly** on edge of base with a strong glue. Decorate edges with holly and ivy. Fill it up with nuts. **If you light the candles, make sure an adult helps you.**

You will need

stiff card   foil   candle

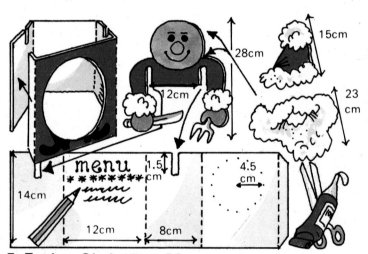

15cm
28cm
12cm
23 cm
1.5 cm
4.5 cm
14cm
menu
12cm   8cm

5. Father Christmas Menu

Cut the box out of card to the sizes shown. Cut out the circle. Write your menu on one side and colour the other side. Fold along dotted lines and glue flap. Cut the beard and hat from paper and colour them. Glue them to the head. Make sure the beard is long enough to hang over and cover the hole. Lift the beard and you see the menu!

6. Christmas Napkin Ring

Paint a toilet roll holder or cover it in paper. Cut out a Father Christmas. Paint him and decorate with glitter and cotton wool. Put your napkin in the roll.

Your Christmas dinner will be all the more fun if you decorate the table with pretty things. Here are some ideas to start you off.

Trace this shape

7. Drink Mat

Trace arrow shape above onto stiff paper 16 times. Cut them out and cover each with coloured foil. Glue them one on top of each other and your mat is ready.

8. Ashtray

Cut slots in a toilet roll holder. Cover all over with foil. Stick a card base **firmly** on it and half fill roll with sand.

9. Christmas Finger Bowl

Cover dish with foil. Decorate with fir and holly. Take a small piece of wood to fit rolled-up paper tissues. Stick small nails at each corner. Put wood and tissues in dish and fill with water. A few slices of lemon in the water and you can clean your greasy fingers!

You will need

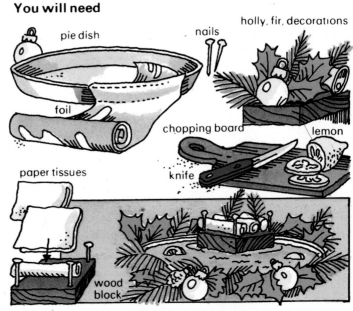

pie dish

nails

holly, fir, decorations

foil

chopping board

lemon

paper tissues

knife

wood block

Christmas Cakes and Biscuits

St Nicholas Letters

Dutch children are given St Nicholas Letter biscuits on December 6th.

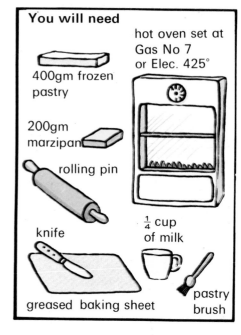

1. Thaw pastry. Roll it out thinly on floured surface. Cut it into strips about 10cm by 4cm.

2. Roll marzipan into 'worms' 10cm long and as thin as your finger.

3. Roll marzipan worms up in the strips of pastry. Dab milk on edges and ends and press to seal them.

4. Shape each pastry roll into a letter. Try IOUSLCPSZ and V first. Seal joins with milk.

5. Use strips of different lengths to make up other letters. Space letters out on a greased baking tray. Brush tops with milk.

6. Bake for 10-15 minutes in oven. Ask a grown-up to help take them out. Let them cool before tasting.

Chocolate Log

In France the traditional Christmas cake is a chocolate log. Here is a way to make an uncooked one.

1. Put the cream, sugar and cocoa in a basin. Whisk cream until it is just stiff enough to stand in peaks.

2. Spread the cream on the biscuits. Sandwich them together in a long roll. Use about half the cream.

3. Wrap the roll of biscuits in foil. Put it in the fridge with the rest of the cream.

4. Next day, unwrap the roll, put it on a plate and cover it with the rest of the cream.

5. Drag a fork over the cream to make 'bark' on the 'log'. Decorate it with icing sugar snow and holly.

6. This cake is rich so serve small slices. Eat it with a fork or spoon. Slices cut at an angle look best.

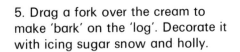

29

Christmas in the Sun

Santa on a surfboard

Christmas always makes people think of snow, reindeer and roast turkey, even if they live in Africa or Australia, where it is hot in December because it is summer.

The shop windows are decorated with artificial snow while people do their Christmas shopping wearing shorts and summer dresses.

There are street carnivals with Santa Claus on his sleigh pulled by reindeer. It is certainly not the right sort of weather for tobogganing. Santa must feel terribly hot, dressed up in a red suit trimmed with fur.

In Mexico there are torchlight processions after dark during the weeks before Christmas. On Christmas Eve there are fireworks as well.

In these countries all the summer flowers can be used in the decorations.

In Australia it is warm enough to sit out of doors at night. Hundreds of people gather in the parks in the big cities and sing carols by candlelight.

A Christmas street carnival on a sunny summer's day

The great feast, which is now our traditional
Christmas dinner with roast turkey, plum pudding and
mince pies, is the kind of meal for people to eat in
winter, not on a hot summer's day. But they do!

In very hot countries they wait until the cooler
evening when they set out the meal on the verandahs
of their bungalows and eat by candlelight.

Many people eat Christmas dinner out of doors. In
Australia, some families take a picnic out into the
garden, the country, or down to the beach. They often
take the whole meal with them, not just turkey
sandwiches. They may even take a small tree complete
with decorations.

Santa Claus visits some of these parties. He has
all sorts of different ways of travelling. In Singapore he
sails in on a catamaran. In California he rides a
surfboard. He is rowed up to Bondi Beach in Australia
in a surfboat. He has even been seen on water skis and
he also uses a carriage pulled by emus.

Christmas dinner on the beach

A Mexican Christmas Eve procession with fireworks and flaming torches

Reindeer Race

Every year, Santa Claus chooses a team of reindeer to draw his sleigh. There is always a tremendous race to be the first to reach him.

Play the Reindeer Race game with your friends. You will need a dice and some counters or buttons. You can make the game very exciting by using two counters each. The first person to get all his counters to Santa is the winner.

Choose between north and south when you get to the middle. Throw the exact number to finish.

Swim across lake. Move on 5 in direction of arrow.

Slip over on ice trying to take short cut. Miss a turn.

You forgot to polish your antlers. Go back 3.

Stop to eat. Miss a turn.

START

Hear someone coming. Hurry on 6 places.

Antlers get tangled in trees Go back 6.

The mountain path is stony and slippery. Go back 1.

Follow the arrow along short cut through forest.

Stop to rest before mountains Miss a turn

Lost in forest. Follow arrow and go round again.

Bob Cratchit's Christmas

This story about a Victorian family's Christmas Day comes from the famous book A Christmas Carol by Charles Dickens. Bob Cratchit was a poor clerk who worked for a mean old man called Ebenezer Scrooge who hated Christmas. One Christmas Eve, Scrooge was haunted by ghosts who showed him what awful things would happen if he went on being mean and miserable at Christmas.

In this part of the story, the Ghost of Christmas Present is showing Scrooge Bob Cratchit's home.

They are not a rich family. There are six children and one of them is a cripple. Their clothes are shabby and there is not a lot to eat—but they are much happier than old Scrooge.

Mrs Cratchit, dressed but poorly in a twice-turned gown, laid the cloth, assisted by Belinda Cratchit, second of her daughters; while Master Peter Cratchit plunged a fork into the saucepan of potatoes, getting the corners of his monstrous shirt collar into his mouth. And now two smaller Cratchits, boy and girl, came tearing in, screaming that outside the baker's they had smelt the goose, and known it for their own; and basking in luxurious thoughts of sage and onion, these young Cratchits danced about the table. Master Peter Cratchit (although his collars nearly choked him) blew the fire, until the slow potatoes bubbling up, knocked loudly at the saucepan lid to be let out and peeled.

'What has ever got your father then?' said Mrs Cratchit. 'And your brother, Tiny Tim! And Martha warn't as late last Christmas Day by half-an-hour!'

'Here's Martha, Mother!' said a girl, appearing as she spoke.

'Here's Martha!' cried the two young Cratchits. 'Hurrah! There's *such* a goose, Martha!'

'Why, bless your heart alive, my dear, how late you are!' said Mrs Cratchit, kissing her a dozen times, and taking off her shawl and bonnet for her.

'We'd a deal of work to finish up last night,' replied the girl, 'and had to clear away this morning, Mother!'

'Well! Never mind so long as you are come,' said Mrs Cratchit. 'Sit ye down before the fire, my dear, and have a warm, Lord bless ye!'

'No, no! There's Father coming!' cried the two young Cratchits, who were everywhere at once. 'Hide, Martha, hide!'

So Martha hid herself, and in came Bob, the father, his threadbare clothes darned and brushed, to look seasonable; and Tiny Tim upon his shoulder. Alas for Tiny Tim, he bore a little crutch, and had his limbs supported by an iron frame!

'Why, where's our Martha?' cried Bob Cratchit, looking round.

'Not coming,' said Mrs Cratchit.

'Not coming!' said Bob. 'Not coming upon Christmas Day!'

Martha didn't like to see him disappointed, so she came out from behind the door, and ran into his arms, while the two young Cratchits hustled Tiny Tim, and bore him off into the wash-house, that he might hear the pudding singing in the copper.

'And how did little Tim behave?' asked Mrs Cratchit, when Bob had hugged his daughter to his heart's content.

'As good as gold,' said Bob, 'and better. Somehow he gets thoughtful, sitting by himself so much, and thinks the strangest things you ever heard. He told me, coming home, that he hoped the people saw him in the church, because he was a cripple, and it might be pleasant to them to remember upon Christmas Day, who made lame beggars walk and blind men see.'

His active little crutch was heard upon the floor, and back came Tiny Tim before another word was spoken, escorted by his brother and sister to his stool before the fire; and while Bob, turning up his cuffs— as if, poor fellow, they were capable of being made more shabby— compounded some hot mixture in a jug with gin and lemons, and stirred it round and round and put it on the hob to simmer, Master Peter and the two young Cratchits went to fetch the goose.

Such a bustle ensued that you might have thought a goose the rarest of all birds; and in truth it was something very like it in that house. Mrs Cratchit made the gravy hissing hot; Master Peter mashed the potatoes with incredible vigour; Miss Belinda sweetened up the apple sauce; Martha dusted the hot plates; Bob took Tiny Tim beside him in a tiny corner at the table; the two young Cratchits set chairs for

everybody, not forgetting themselves, and mounting guard upon their posts, crammed spoons into their mouths, lest they should shriek for goose before their turn came to be helped. At last the dishes were set on, and grace was said. It was succeeded by a breathless pause, as Mrs Cratchit, looking slowly all along the carving-knife, prepared to plunge it in the breast; but when she did, and when the long-expected gush of stuffing issued forth, one murmur of delight arose all round the board, and even Tiny Tim, excited by the two young Cratchits, beat on the table with the handle of his knife, and feebly cried Hurrah!

There never was such a goose. Bob said he didn't believe there ever was such a goose cooked. Its tenderness and flavour, size and cheapness, were the themes of universal admiration. Eked out by the apple sauce and mashed potatoes, it was a sufficient dinner for the whole family; indeed, as Mrs Cratchit said with great delight (surveying one small atom of a bone upon the dish), they hadn't ate it all at last! Yet everyone had had enough, and the youngest Cratchits, in particular, were steeped in sage and onion to the eyebrows! But now, the plates being changed by Miss Belinda, Mrs Cratchit left the room alone—too nervous to bear

witnesses—to take the pudding up and bring it in.

Suppose it should not be done enough! Suppose it should break in turning out! Suppose somebody should have got over the wall of the backyard, and stolen it, while they were merry with the goose—a supposition at which the two young Cratchits became livid! All sorts of horrors were supposed.

Halloa! A great deal of steam! The pudding was out of the copper. A smell like a washing-day! That was the cloth. A smell like an eating-house and a pastry-cook's next door to each other, with a laundress's next door to that! That was the pudding! In half a minute Mrs Cratchit entered—flushed, but smiling proudly—with the pudding, like a speckled cannonball, so hard and firm, blazing in ignited brandy, with holly stuck into the top.

Oh, a wonderful pudding! Everybody had something to say about it, but nobody said it was at all a small pudding for a large family. Any Cratchit would have blushed to hint at such a thing.

At last the dinner was all done, the cloth was cleared, the hearth swept, and the fire made up. The compound in the jug being tasted, and considered perfect, apples and oranges were put upon the table, and

a shovelful of chestnuts on the fire. Then all the Cratchit family drew round the hearth in what Bob Cratchit called a circle, meaning half a one; and at Bob Cratchit's elbow stood the family display of glass. Two tumblers, and a custard-cup without a handle.

These held the hot stuff from the jug, however, as well as golden goblets would have done; and Bob served it out with beaming looks, while the chestnuts on the fire sputtered and cracked noisily. Then Bob proposed:

'A Merry Christmas to us all, my dears. God bless us!'

Which all the family re-echoed.

'God bless us every one!' said Tiny Tim, the last of all.

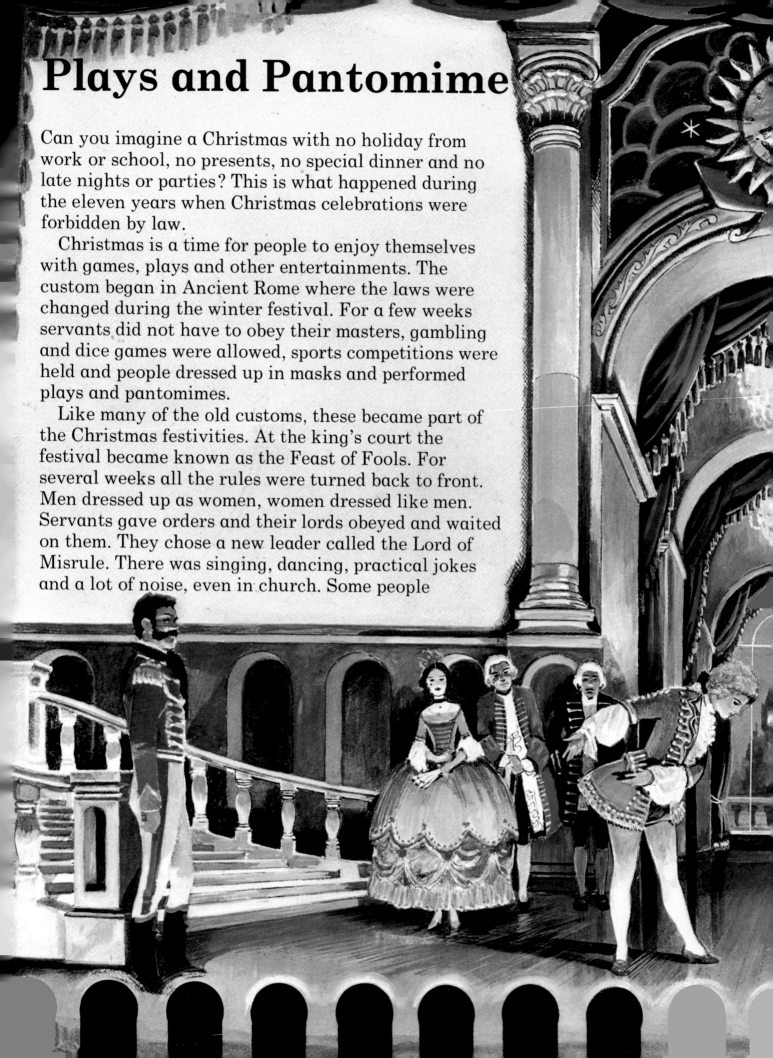

Plays and Pantomime

Can you imagine a Christmas with no holiday from work or school, no presents, no special dinner and no late nights or parties? This is what happened during the eleven years when Christmas celebrations were forbidden by law.

Christmas is a time for people to enjoy themselves with games, plays and other entertainments. The custom began in Ancient Rome where the laws were changed during the winter festival. For a few weeks servants did not have to obey their masters, gambling and dice games were allowed, sports competitions were held and people dressed up in masks and performed plays and pantomimes.

Like many of the old customs, these became part of the Christmas festivities. At the king's court the festival became known as the Feast of Fools. For several weeks all the rules were turned back to front. Men dressed up as women, women dressed like men. Servants gave orders and their lords obeyed and waited on them. They chose a new leader called the Lord of Misrule. There was singing, dancing, practical jokes and a lot of noise, even in church. Some people

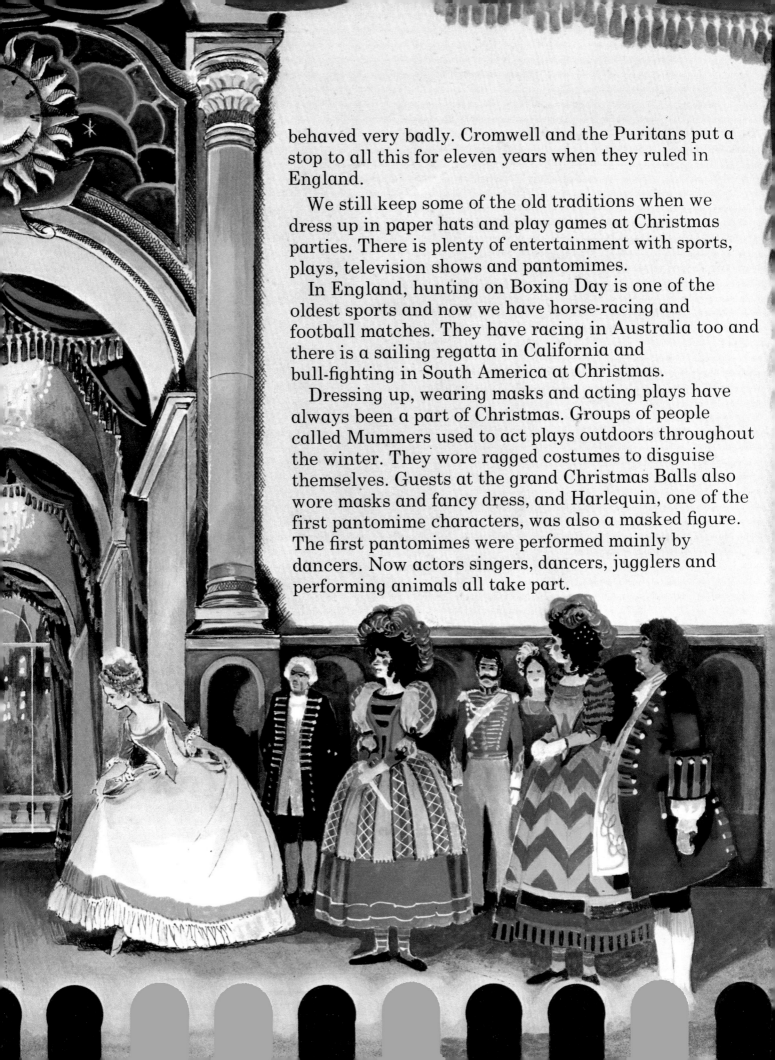

behaved very badly. Cromwell and the Puritans put a stop to all this for eleven years when they ruled in England.

We still keep some of the old traditions when we dress up in paper hats and play games at Christmas parties. There is plenty of entertainment with sports, plays, television shows and pantomimes.

In England, hunting on Boxing Day is one of the oldest sports and now we have horse-racing and football matches. They have racing in Australia too and there is a sailing regatta in California and bull-fighting in South America at Christmas.

Dressing up, wearing masks and acting plays have always been a part of Christmas. Groups of people called Mummers used to act plays outdoors throughout the winter. They wore ragged costumes to disguise themselves. Guests at the grand Christmas Balls also wore masks and fancy dress, and Harlequin, one of the first pantomime characters, was also a masked figure. The first pantomimes were performed mainly by dancers. Now actors singers, dancers, jugglers and performing animals all take part.

Pantomime Puzzle

In the theatre the Christmas pantomime still includes many of the old traditions. Pantomime means 'all in mime', that is acting without any words. The plot of the pantomime is usually a fairy story. There is always a man in it dressed up as an old lady. The hero is always played by a girl, called the principal boy. The hero or heroine usually begins as a poor unlucky person but ends up rich and famous. This way of turning things upside down is all that is left of the Feast of Fools.

Match these people with the words opposite

1. DLNDIAA NDA IHS IACMG PLMA
2. EEIGNPLS YAUEBT
3. AAEKTLBSN EHT NDA KJCA
4. FWLO RFMO EILLTT EDR IIGNRD ODOH
5. LYGU EITSSSR OMFR AEEILDCNLR
6. OIOU-SS-BSNTP
7. UUYYHD-TTPPMM

Answers on page 48

A Christmas King
in a Paper Crown

by Richard Blythe

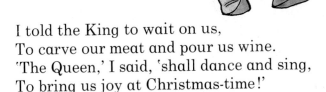

At topsy-turvy Christmas-time,
A-many, many years ago,
For twelve short days I ruled the Court
And told my lords what each must do!

They took my greasy apron off,
They put a crown upon my head.
They laid a sceptre in my hand,
And dressed me royally, in red.

They set me on a Christmas throne,
For twice six days to make the law.
'My Lord Misrule,' they greeted me,
Like subjects, kneeling on the floor!

Yes, down they knelt—the King, his Queen,
Their lords and ladies bold and fair.
They made me King of Christmas-time,
And knelt to do me honour there.

At topsy-turvy Christmas-time
They watched me, should I smile or frown.
For servants were the masters then,
And all the Court was upside-down!

I told the King to wait on us,
To carve our meat and pour us wine.
'The Queen,' I said, 'shall dance and sing,
To bring us joy at Christmas-time!'

I told six Earls to play a dance
For cook and groom and serving-maid.
I told three Dukes to brush the hearth
And see our fire was brightly laid.

'Each lord,' I said, 'shall wear a dress.
Their ladies, they must dress as lords.
You servants, wear your masters' clothes,
Their buckled shoes and silver swords!'

At topsy-turvy Christmas-time,
With sceptre, robe and paper crown,
For twelve short days I turned the Court
First inside-out, then upside-down!

New Year

Old Father Time brings in the young New Year

New Year is the time to make a fresh start with some good resolutions. Promise yourself that you will do certain things better in the New Year. In many countries it is the time to settle debts. In France and Germany, New Year's Day is a time for visiting and grown-ups give each other presents.

New Year's Eve is a time for parties. In Austria someone dresses up as an old man called Sylvester. He wears mistletoe in his hair and goes around kissing all the girls. In Germany they play fortune-telling games. Some people sit around the fire telling ghost stories while they wait for the clock to strike midnight. Others drink and sing in the streets. In Switzerland there are bell-ringing competitions. All this noise was supposed to drive away evil spirits.

In some countries farmers go out to the orchards and wassail the fruit trees. They sing and shout and drink their health. Sometimes they fire shots into the branches. This is supposed to wake up the trees and

Wassailing the fruit trees

New Year street celebrations

40

drive away evil spirits so that they will bear a good crop of fruit next year.

Even if people do not believe in the old superstitions, they enjoy keeping up these traditions.

At midnight church bells are rung all around the world. In Paris, car drivers hoot their horns. In the harbours, the ships' sirens are sounded.

Everybody should say 'Happy New Year' to the people around them, even if they are strangers.

In Scotland, New Year's Eve is called Hogmanay. After midnight young men go first-footing. The custom gets its name because the first person to set foot in a house in the New Year is supposed to bring good luck. The visitor must have dark hair and bring a present with them. A man with red hair, or any woman, would bring bad luck.

Chinese New Year is celebrated on a different day each year. They have fantastic street processions, with masks, fireworks and huge paper dragons.

Ringing in the New Year

First-footing at Hogmanay

Chinese New Year celebrations

Party Games

Christmas has always been a time for fun and games.. Hundreds of years ago, there were laws forbidding people to gamble or play games with cards or dice for most of the year. But at Christmas these laws were lifted so people gave parties and enjoyed themselves as much as possible for this short time.

People used to dress up, sing, dance, ring bells and let off fireworks. We still dress up in paper hats and make a lot of noise with whistles, hooters and bangs from crackers.

Here are some traditional games from around the world which you might like to play at your Christmas party.

Capture the Star

In Alaska people play a Christmas game called Capture the Star. They dress up as the Three Kings and their servants and carry a star from house to house, singing carols. Other children dress up as Herod's soldiers and chase after them and try to capture the star.

Round Song

... On the First day of Christmas
My true love sent to me
A Partridge in a Pear Tree ...

Singing songs like this was an old Christmas game. People took turns to sing a verse. Each person had to add a new line and remember all that had gone before.

Play this game at your party. Sit in a circle and take turns to sing a verse. Make up your own words. Each person must think of a new 'gift' and add it to the list.

See how many verses you can sing before people start forgetting the gifts. When some one makes a mistake they are 'out'. The last person should get a prize.

Your song might go like this
... On the Third Day of Christmas
My true love sent to me
Three Blind Mice
Two Tiny Turtles
And a Partridge in a Pear Tree! ...

Dutch Pass the Parcel

In the Netherlands they have a special way of wrapping up parcels. They wrap each present in layers and layers of paper with a rhyme or riddle attached to each wrapper. The riddle gives a clue to what is in the parcel and who it is for. Everyone helps to unwrap it and tries to guess the answer.

Why not make up a parcel like this for a game of Pass the Parcel. Any one guessing a riddle should get a sweet as a prize.

Ask a grown-up to play some music on a piano, record or cassette. Sit in a circle and pass the parcel round When the music stops, the person holding the parcel should unwrap a layer and guess at the riddle.

Answers on page 48

1. Half of me is a little dog

2. Half of me is your favourite animal

3. Your fingers will bring me to life.

4. I work in a theatre.

Don't forget to tidy up

Mexican Pinatas

In Mexico, children get lots of surprise parcels at Christmas. They are called pinatas. The parcels are hung up high and the children hit them with sticks to break them open. Some pinatas contain nice surprises such as sweets or little presents. But others have nasty surprises in instead. When they are broken the children are showered with bits of paper, feathers, beans, or even water.

Make some pinatas up for your party. Decorate large paper bags, Half fill each one with a different surprise. Put wrapped sweets in one, scraps of paper in another, dried peas in another and so on. In the biggest one put tiny presents such as paper hats, whistles and hooters. Tie the bags up with string and hang them up around the house, or across a room on a string.

Breaking the pinatas would be a good game to end your party.

The Three Kings

January 6 is called the Epiphany. It is a great feast day in Italy, Spain and many other countries. This is the time when the children there get presents in memory of the gifts brought to the Christ Child by the Three Kings. These kings were three wise men who followed a star to Bethlehem. Their names were Caspar, Melchior and Balthazar. They brought valuable gifts of gold, myrrh, which was a scented ointment, and frankincense, which was precious oil. In Spain and France the children go out to look for the Kings, taking gifts of hay for the camels. In Germany boys dress up as kings and carry a star round the village, singing carols.

In France and other countries families used to have a Three Kings Cake with a bean hidden in it. Whoever found the bean in their slice was made King, or Queen, for the day.

Another name for this day is Twelfth Day. It is the last of the Twelve Days of Christmas which used to be one long holiday. Twelfth Night parties were very noisy. It was the last night of the Feast of Fools before the Lord of Misrule had to give up his crown and become a servant again.

Twelfth Night is the time when all the decorations should be taken down or else they will bring bad luck. All the sweets decorating the tree can be eaten—if there are any left! In some cities in America, they collect all the old trees and burn them on a huge bonfire. Artificial trees have to be folded up and packed away with the lights and decorations until next Christmas.

Myrrh and frankincense come from these plants.
Gold was made into jewelry and coins.

The First Day of Christmas

Nowadays, Christmas cards, decorations and gifts appear in the shops early in autumn. But we do not have such a long holiday at Christmas itself as people had long ago. At one time, the celebrations, fairs and feasts went on for twelve days and nights until January 6.

People gave gifts such as home-made sweets, cakes, fruit or birds and animals caught while hunting. Very little work was done, many rules and laws were ignored and there was lots of singing and dancing.

In the song The First Day of Christmas, the new line in each verse tells of an amazing gift that a lady was sent each day. With such a long Christmas, all the birds would have been useful food; people used to eat swans and colly birds (blackbirds) in those days. The drummers and pipers would play for the merry-makers.

After each new line, sing all the other lines that came before.

1 The first day of Christmas, my true love sent to me
A partridge in a pear tree.
2 The second day of Christmas, my true love sent to me
Two turtle doves and a partridge in a pear tree.
3 The third day of Christmas, my true love sent to me
Three French hens, two turtle doves and a partridge in a pear tree.
4 The fourth day of Christmas, my true love sent to me
Four colly birds, three French hens, and so on.
5 The fifth day of Christmas, my true love sent to me
Five gold rings, four colly birds, and so on.
6 The sixth day of Christmas, my true love sent to me
Six geese a-laying, five gold rings, and so on.
7 The seventh day of Christmas, my true love sent to me
Seven swans a-swimming, six geese a-laying, and so on.

8 The eighth day of Christmas, my true love sent to me
Eight maids a-milking, seven swans a-swimming, and so on.
9 The ninth day of Christmas, my true love sent to me
Nine drummers drumming, eight maids a-milking, and so on.
10 The tenth day of Christmas, my true love sent to me
Ten pipers piping, nine drummers drumming, and so on.
11 The eleventh day of Christmas, my true love sent to me
Eleven ladies dancing, ten pipers piping, and so on.
12 The twelfth day of Christmas, my true love sent to me
Twelve lords a-leaping, eleven ladies dancing, ten pipers piping, nine drummers drumming, eight maids a-milking, seven swans a-swimming, six geese a-laying, five gold rings, four colly birds, three French hens, two turtle doves and a partridge in a pear tree.

Index

Answers

Page 38 Pantomime Puzzle
E=1   ALADDIN AND HIS MAGIC LAMP
B=2   SLEEPING BEAUTY
G=3   JACK AND THE BEANSTALK
A=4   WOLF FROM LITTLE RED RIDING HOOD
D=5   UGLY SISTERS FROM CINDERELLA
C=6   PUSS-IN-BOOTS
F=7   HUMPTY-DUMPTY

Page 43 Pass the Parcel
A puppet